16.95

# COMMUNITY CONNECTIONS ?

## WHAT DO THEY DO?

# POLICE OFFICERS

BY GAETANO CAPICI

Published in the United States of America by Cherry Lake Publishing
Ann Arbor, Michigan
www.cherrylakepublishing.com

Content Adviser: Bryce Kolpack, Associate Dean, Public Safety Division, Northcentral Technical College
Reading Adviser: Cecilia Minden-Cupp, PhD, Literacy Consultant

Photo Credits: Cover and page 1, ©Radius Images/Alamy; page 5, ©Kellyoptra/Dreamstime. com; page 7, ©iStockphoto.com/Maxfocus; page 9, ©iStockphoto.com/Tashka; page 11, ©Hhltdave5/Dreamstime.com; page 13, ©Simone van den Berg, used under license from Shutterstock, Inc.; page 15, ©iStockphoto.com/jtyler; page 17, ©iStockphoto.com/ftwitty; page 19, ©David R. Frazier Photolibrary, Inc./Alamy; page 21, ©Hermgell/Dreamstime.com

**LIBRARY OF CONGRESS CATALOGING-IN-PUBLICATION DATA**
Capici, Gaetano, 1985–
  What do they do? Police officers / by Gaetano Capici.
    p. cm.—(Community connections)
  Includes bibliographical references and index.
  ISBN-13: 978-1-60279-803-8 (lib. bdg.)
  ISBN-10: 1-60279-803-6 (lib. bdg.)
  1. Police—Juvenile literature. I. Title. II. Title: Police officers.
III. Series.
  HV7922.C35 2011
  363.2'3—dc22                          2009042799

Cherry Lake Publishing would like to acknowledge the work of The Partnership for 21st Century Skills. Please visit www.21stcenturyskills.org for more information.

Printed in the United States of America
Corporate Graphics Inc.
July 2010
CLFA07

POLICE OFFICERS

# CONTENTS

WHAT DO THEY DO?

# ON THE LOOKOUT

It's a beautiful day for flying a kite in the park. You're having a lot of fun. Then you notice something. Your little brother has wandered too far away. You can't find him. Who's that down the path? A police officer! He helps your worried family find your brother. He is safe!

Police officers often help lost children.

Police officers serve us in many ways. They **patrol** different parts of town. They often ride in police cars. The cars have **sirens** and flashing warning lights. Officers patrol alone or with **partners**. They look for anything that doesn't seem right. Sometimes, they spot stolen cars. They also break up fights.

Police officers sometimes patrol on horseback.

**THINK!**

Some police officers work at night. Some work on weekends. Some work during holidays. Why do you think that is? Here's a hint: Think about what police officers do. Does their work ever end? Do we always need to be kept safe?

Police officers might have **traffic** duties. They give **tickets** to people who break the law when they drive. Has there been a car accident? Officers are on the way! They try to learn exactly what happened. They also direct traffic. They help keep cars and trucks moving along.

Some police officers direct traffic.

# FIGHTING CRIME

Who rushes to help when there is trouble? Police officers! **Dispatchers** use computers and radios to reach them. They tell the officers where help is needed and why. What if someone robbed a store? Officers arrive quickly. Their work can be **dangerous**. They **investigate** the crime. They want to catch the thief.

Dispatchers talk to officers through radios and computers.

There are many kinds of police officers. **Detectives** solve crimes after they have happened. They search for clues. Detectives do not wear police uniforms.

Other special officers know about **bombs**. They can keep them from exploding.

Some police officers work in neighborhoods. They help people keep their homes safe.

Detectives investigate places where crimes have taken place.

CREATE!

What makes someone a good police officer? Being brave? Being smart? Being curious? Make a list of five qualities that officers should have. Write why they are good qualities, too. Have you learned more about police officers?

13

Some officers have special partners to help fight crime. They are police dogs. They search for people who are hiding or are missing. How? Police dogs have a strong sense of smell. They can see and hear well. They're fast. These skills help the dogs track down drugs or bombs, too.

Police dogs help sniff out dangerous materials.

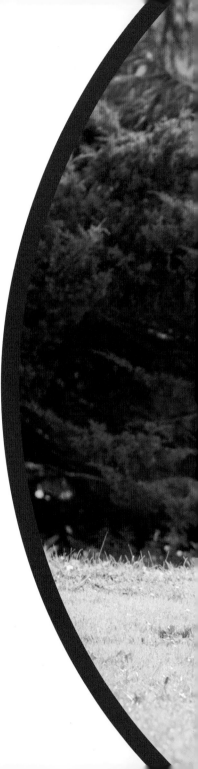

# OTHER DUTIES

Police officers stay busy all day. They write up many reports. They keep records of what happens. This is because officers sometimes have to go to court. They explain their cases. Good records help them remember what happened.

Police officers keep records of everything they do.

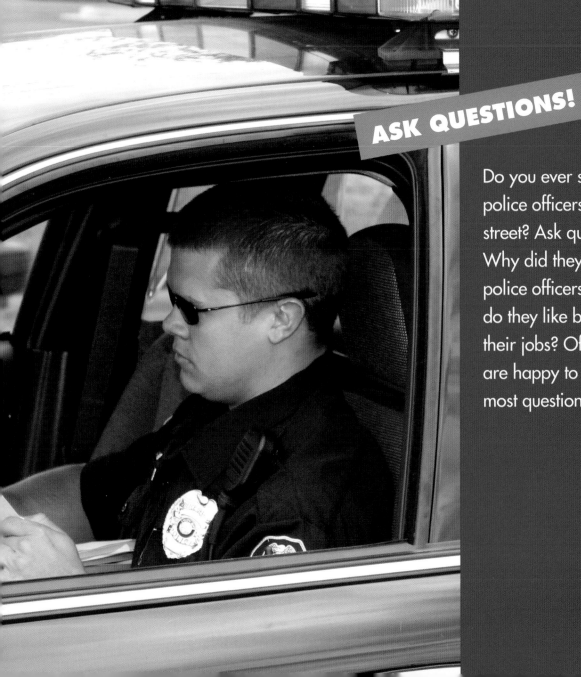

Do you ever see police officers on the street? Ask questions! Why did they become police officers? What do they like best about their jobs? Officers are happy to answer most questions.

17

Has a police officer ever visited your school? Did she speak to your class? Many officers enjoy teaching children about ways to stay safe. They may talk about drugs. They may also talk about being safe around strangers.

Police officers often give advice to kids about staying safe.

Officers might help people who are hurt. They give them first aid. Sometimes, officers control large crowds.

Being a police officer is a busy job. All police officers have something in common. They like to help people and keep them safe!

20

Some police officers make amazing rescues!

# GLOSSARY

**bombs** (BOMZ) containers filled with materials that can explode

**dangerous** (DAYN-jur-uhss) likely to cause harm

**detectives** (di-TEK-tivz) officers who study clues in order to solve crimes after they happen

**dispatchers** (diss-PACH-urz) people who send police officers where they are needed

**investigate** (in-VESS-tuh-gate) to find out about something

**partners** (PART-nurz) people who do something together

**patrol** (puh-TROHL) to travel through an area often in order to keep it safe

**sirens** (SYE-runz) devices that make loud sounds

**tickets** (TIK-itss) written orders to go to court or pay a fine

**traffic** (TRAF-ik) the movement of cars or people along a path

# FIND OUT MORE

## BOOKS

Gonzalez, Lissette. *Police in Action*. New York: PowerKids Press, 2008.

Kenney, Karen L. *Police Officers at Work*. Edina, MN: Magic Wagon, 2010.

## WEB SITES

**Job Futures—Service Canada: Police Officers**
*www.jobfutures.ca/noc/6261.shtml*
Learn about being a police officer in Canada.

**United States Department of Labor—Bureau of Labor Statistics: Police Officer**
*www.bls.gov/k12/law01.htm*
Look here for more information about the jobs of U.S. police officers.

# INDEX

## ABOUT THE AUTHOR

Gaetano Capici graduated from DePaul University with bachelor's degrees in English and Spanish. He lives near Chicago, Illinois. He thanks all law enforcement officers who work hard to keep us safe.

24